Home Green Home

Tyler Schumacher

Contents

Rigby
A Harcourt Achieve Imprint

www.Rigby.com
1-800-531-5015

Your Amazing Home

If you stop to think about it, your house is a pretty amazing place. Besides sheltering you from the weather, it provides you with light, clean water, and a place to store your food and belongings. It gives you a place to prepare meals and clean up when you are done.

If you are like many other people, your house keeps you cool in the summer and warm in the winter. It might even have a place for you to wash your clothes. All this in one building!

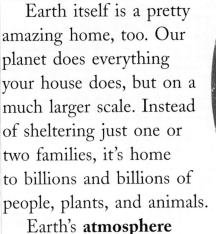

Earth itself is a pretty amazing home, too. Our planet does everything your house does, but on a much larger scale. Instead of sheltering just one or two families, it's home to billions and billions of people, plants, and animals.

Earth's **atmosphere** collects the sun's heat, providing protection from the extreme cold of outer space. Plants grow in Earth's soil, giving people and animals food to eat. Earth's lakes and rivers provide fresh water for drinking and cleaning. All this on one planet!

So you actually have two amazing homes: your own house and Earth. Both of them give what you need to survive, and both of them require care and respect. But, sadly, some houses that provide shelter for people don't do a good job of caring for everyone's larger home, Earth. Many houses mistreat Earth by using large amounts of energy and producing great quantities of waste.

The electricity that lights most homes comes from power plants. These power plants burn coal, which releases harmful gases into the air, as do the oil and gas that heat many of our homes. Fuels such as coal, oil, and natural gas are **nonrenewable resources**, which means that once they are used up, they cannot be replaced.

The carpets and paints used in many houses sometimes contain chemicals that can be harmful to both people and Earth. Many homeowners waste large amounts of water when watering their lawns or taking long showers. Household items that could be recycled are sometimes thrown into **landfills.**

Green Homes

To try to address these problems, some people have built homes that are friendlier to the health of both people and Earth. These houses are known as *green* homes. Green homes do three things very well: they reduce, reuse, and recycle. To reduce means to use less of something, such as electricity. To reuse is to find a second use for something, such as using a glass jar to hold pencils. To recycle is to break something down and remake its materials into something else, such as making old newspapers into paper napkins.

More and more people are recycling glass bottles, plastic containers, and aluminum cans.

WE RECYCLE

Green homes reduce the use of resources in a variety of ways. They reduce the use of potentially polluting forms of energy like coal or oil by creating energy from renewable sources, such as sunlight or wind. They reduce the amount of water they use and the waste they create. Green homes are sometimes constructed from reused materials like wood, glass, and metal. And green homes often contain recycled materials, such as special concrete made from old computer parts.

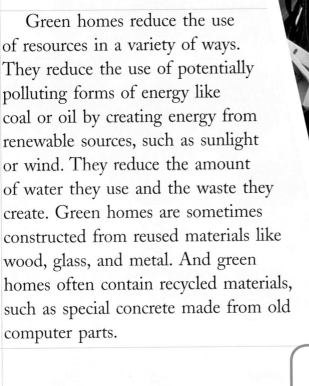

If they are not recycled, old computers will take up a lot of space in landfills.

David Hertz, his wife Stacy Fong, and their three children, Collin, Sophie, and Max, live in a green home. David and Stacy are architects, which means they design houses and other buildings.

David grew up surfing the waves near Santa Monica and Malibu, California. He developed a love for nature, both in and out of the ocean. After watching the waste from oil refineries and power plants pollute much of Santa Monica Bay, he decided to do something about it. After finishing architecture school, he set out to design green buildings, and in 1998, he decided to build a green home for his family.

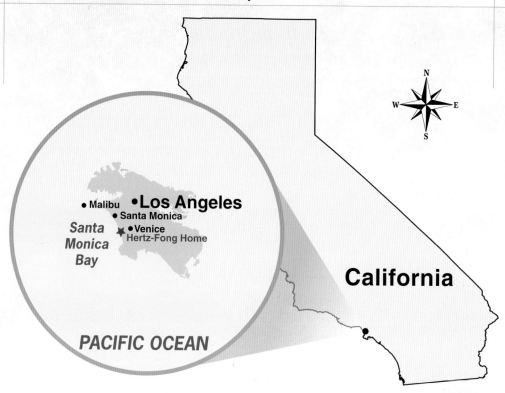

The Hertz-Fong home sits on a quiet street, just blocks from the Pacific Ocean. Four bright buildings, a large courtyard with a swimming pool in the middle, a fire pit, and a fountain make it look like a tropical vacation spot. Bridges connect the four buildings, while a sleeping porch provides a cozy spot for comfortable summer nights.

The home started as one building and a garage. When the house next door came up for sale, the family purchased it and created a new house for guests, a studio, and a pool.

The Hertz-Fong home is eye-catching as you approach it from the street.

Collin, Sophie, and Max enjoy many of the same activities as other kids. Collin likes playing in his band and making models, while Sophie enjoys volleyball and art. Max likes computers, and someday he hopes to be a cartoonist. Their home, however, is not like very many others. You can see examples of reducing, reusing, and recycling all around their home.

Although their home is quite different from most homes, the Hertz-Fong family enjoys a comfortable living space.

Reducing the Use of Electricity and Fuel

Every morning, the inside of the Hertz-Fong home brightens with the rising sun. Many windows line the walls, but none of them have curtains. David designed the home so that almost everywhere you look, you can see the outside. Collin especially likes the windows because they allow him to see the stars at night.

But there is another reason Collin likes the windows in his home. The natural sunlight that shines through them reduces the need for electric lights. Half the electricity made in the U.S. is produced in power plants that burn coal. When power plants burn coal, they release harmful pollution into the air. By using less electricity from power plants, the Hertz-Fong home plays less of a role in creating air pollution, and that allows everyone to breathe easier.

The home's large windows make it hard to tell the difference between the inside and the outside.

Don't worry—the family doesn't live completely without electricity. They let the sun make it for them! Whether it's Sophie writing a paper on the computer or Collin listening to a compact disc on the stereo, the family uses electricity produced by the power of the sun. How? David installed **photovoltaic** panels on the roof that capture the bright California sunshine and **convert** it into electricity. On a clear day, the sun powers all their lights, computers, and machines such as their washing machine and refrigerator.

The California climate is perfect for the use of photovoltaic panels. What other parts of the country might be good locations for photovoltaic panels? Why?

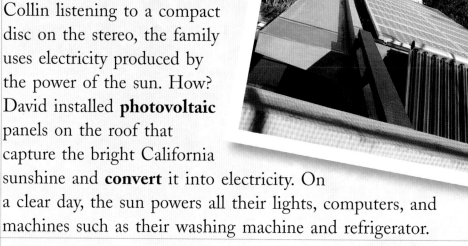

Photovoltaic panels are like huge, flat batteries that store the sun's energy as electricity.

To help the children understand how the family's green electrical system works, David showed them the home's electric meter. When the meter runs in one direction, the family is using power from a power plant, which is how most homes work. But when the sun gets bright enough, the meter runs in the opposite direction. That means the family is making its own electricity, with enough left over to sell back to the company that owns the power plant. The family is making money from the sun and reducing air pollution at the same time!

How Photovoltaic Panels Help Reduce Air Pollution

If a green house uses photovoltaic panels...

⇩

then it uses less electricity generated by a power plant.

⇩

If less electricity from a power plant is used...

⇩

then the power plants burn less coal.

⇩

If less coal is burnt at power plants...

⇩

then fewer harmful pollutants from the coal enter the air.

⇩

If fewer harmful pollutants enter the air...

⇩

then people breathe cleaner air.

One thing Max really likes about his house is its concrete floor. Concrete usually feels cold to the touch. But in this house, it not only feels warm, it also provides heat to the home. Tubes buried inside the floor **circulate** hot water while sunlight heats and pumps this water throughout the home. This makes for toasty toes and allows the family to walk around barefoot all year. It also allows them to reduce their use of natural gas for heating. Sophie likes the floors too, but mostly because she can in-line skate inside the house!

This concrete floor is also a heater!

The heated floor also means that there's no need for carpet. This is healthier for the family and Earth, since some carpeting contains **toxic** chemicals and can provide a living place for molds, dust, and tiny harmful creatures. Using **radiant** heating like the tubes inside the concrete floor also means that no ducts have to be built in the walls. Ducts are the shafts that circulate warm or cool air. But ducts can also house mold and dust. Not having ducts reduces the amount of air pollution inside the house.

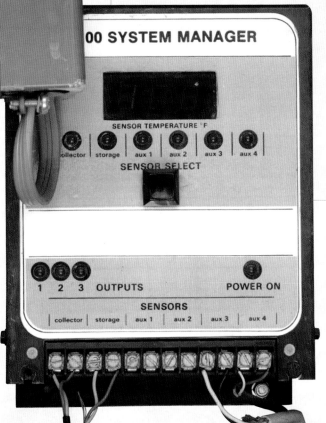

00 SYSTEM MANAGER

SENSOR TEMPERATURE °F

collector | storage | aux 1 | aux 2 | aux 3 | aux 4

SENSOR SELECT

1   2   3   OUTPUTS   POWER ON

SENSORS

| collector | storage | aux 1 | aux 2 | aux 3 | aux 4 |

The family's electric meter is actually a part-time money-maker.

The Hertz-Fong air conditioner is made up of a system of vents and windows.

While it might seem reasonable that the sun can provide the home's heat, surprisingly, the sun can also do the cooling! How? On most days along California's sea coast, a cool breeze blows in off the ocean. David saw this steady breeze as a great way to provide natural air conditioning to his home. This gentle wind is cleaner—and much cheaper—than the air blown by an electric air conditioner. An electric air conditioner can be very expensive to run during hot California summers.

In order to take advantage of the sea breeze, David designed a house that catches the wind from the outside to **funnel** it inside. By opening the right combination of doors and windows—some of which even open automatically in the heat—warm air rises and escapes. As the warm air drifts up and out, cool breezes whisk through the home's rooms and hallways. During the home's construction, David used smoke to test how the air circulated. The smoke made it possible for him to see how breezes would travel through the house.

Architects like David Hertz sometimes use smoke to see how air circulates in the buildings they design.

Reducing Harmful Chemicals

If you have ever smelled fresh paint, you know that if you are not careful, the fumes can give you headaches, make you dizzy, or sometimes make you just plain sick. The ingredients that make wet paint so smelly are chemicals called **volatile organic compounds**, or VOCs. VOCs can give off harmful fumes long after the paint has dried. Many house paints, even ones meant for indoor use, contain VOCs. To reduce these types of unhealthy fumes, David decided to coat the inside walls of his house with a special paint that contained no VOCs.

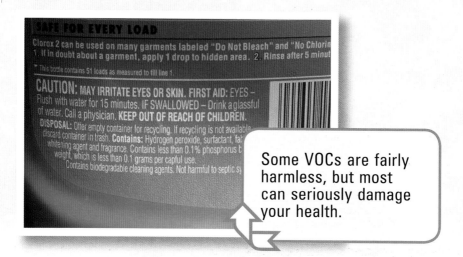

Some VOCs are fairly harmless, but most can seriously damage your health.

The family also wanted to reduce the amount of money it would have to spend on outdoor paint during the home's life. Because of the effects of sunlight and weather, most homes need a coat of outdoor paint every few years. However, the Hertz-Fong family discovered a way to protect the outside of their house without having to repaint it often. Batches of stucco—a mixture of plaster and sand—were mixed with natural dyes and smeared onto the walls. This mixture dried to provide a colored finish that will never need to be repainted.

The natural materials used in much of the Hertz-Fong home never need painting.

The Hertz-Fong family also cleans its home in a green way. They do this by avoiding the use of chemical cleaners, many of which contain bleach or other substances that can be harmful to humans. Not only can these cleaners be bad for people, they sometimes wash down drains and end up in local streams or lakes. This polluted water can harm plants and wildlife.

One way the family reduces its need for chemical cleaners is by having concrete floors. Spilled milk, dropped food, or tracked-in dirt can be easily wiped up to keep the floors clean. There is no need for chemical stain removers for the carpets, because there aren't any carpets!

Chemicals used for cleaning can poison rivers, lakes and streams.

When the family does need to seriously clean something, they use mixtures of vinegar, baking soda, and plain water. These mixtures do a fine job and can be used to clean just about anything. Choosing not to use chemical cleaners means the Hertz-Fong home remains a happier and healthier place.

Natural cleaning products like these make chemical cleaners unnecessary.

A "Green" Pool

The family's swimming pool rests in the middle of the main courtyard. Even though California is warm throughout the year, nights and some winter days can be cool. Luckily for Collin, Sophie, and Max, their father came up with a way to keep the pool warm enough for swimming while still reducing energy use.

David built a layer of **insulation** around the inside of the pool so that it would hold heat better. Next, he made the pool shallow and gave it a dark-colored bottom surface. Shallow water warms up faster than deep water, and dark colors absorb more energy from the sun than light colors. Both of these features help to keep the pool water warm.

One of the nicest features of the Hertz-Fong home, the family's pool requires no electricity to be kept warm.

22

The rest of the pool's heating comes from—you guessed it—the sun. Water is pumped from the pool onto the roof, where it runs through special tubes that catch the sun's rays. The sun provides enough direct energy to keep the pool warm for about nine months out of the year. During the winter months, the family uses small amounts of natural gas to heat the pool's water. However, their gas bills are only about 1/6th of the amount they were before they installed a **solar heat** system.

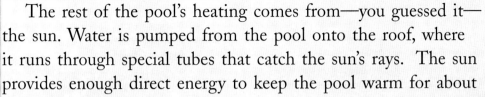

The pool's cover keeps leaves and dirt out of the water, so the pool stays cleaner. It also helps the pool retain heat when not in use.

The Hertz-Fong swimming pool uses none of the harmful chemicals that most pools contain, such as bromine or chlorine. These chemicals—which kill bacteria and other germs—can make a person's skin or eyes itchy and red. When the Hertz-Fong children experienced these reactions to pool chemicals, David and Stacy decided to keep their pool clean and safe without the use of harsh chemicals.

Bacteria such as *e. coli* are controlled without the use of chemicals in the Hertz-Fong pool.

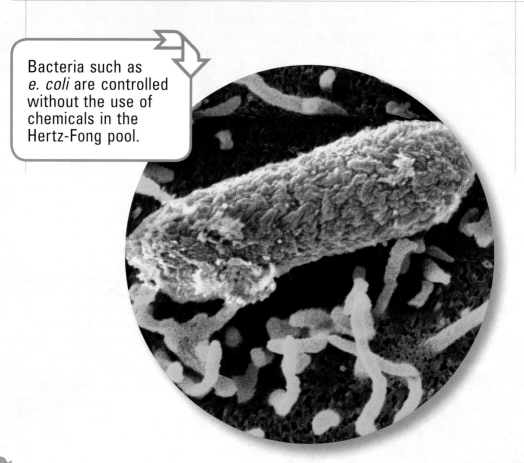

A special system using an **ionizer** and an **ozone generator** keeps their pool clean. The ionizer works by using a small electrical current along with silver and copper to kill bacteria, algae, and viruses. The ozone generator kills **microorganisms** by changing some of the oxygen in the water into a form called ozone. Together, they clean the pool's water without the use of any harmful chemicals.

Max, Sophie, and Collin used to rinse off after getting out of the pool because they wanted to make sure they got all the chemicals off their skin. Now, they rinse off before jumping into the pool because the pool is cleaner than they are!

Swimmers keep pool water clean by showering *before* they enter the pool.

Reducing the Use of Water

Did you know that 97% of Earth's water is salt water? Of the 3% that is fresh, less than 1% is clean and safe enough for human use. In some parts of the world, people use much more water than can be replaced by rainfall. In California, where the Hertz-Fong family lives along with about 36 million other people, it only rains about 14 inches a year. That means reducing water usage in their region is very important.

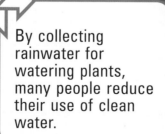

By collecting rainwater for watering plants, many people reduce their use of clean water.

One way the family reduces its use of water is by watering their plants with stored rainwater. The patio is built to gather rain into two underground tanks, each one holding many gallons. When the water is needed, the water is pumped out and used to water the family's plants.

The family also chose their plants based on their knowledge of local rainfall amounts. Since California is so dry, the family selected plants that don't need much water.

Reusing and Recycling Materials

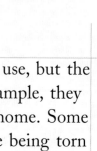

The Hertz-Fong family reduces energy and water use, but the family also does a good job of reusing things. For example, they reused many different materials when building their home. Some of the solar panels came off other buildings that were being torn down or remodeled. The light fixtures in their office and kitchen came from old U.S. Navy ships. When David built the home's doors, he reused the leftover wood scraps to make a table.

When pouring the concrete for their home, lumber was used to form it into shape. David reused this wood to help build some of the home's walls. Also, a wall that runs along part of their property is made from leftover dirt and sand. To build this special kind of wall, known as a rammed-earth wall because it is made of packed dirt, David used lumber to hold the dirt in place until it hardened. Later, he reused this wood to build a deck for the front yard.

By building a wall of packed dirt, Hertz saved on use of lumber in his home.

Someone is planning to reuse an entire house!

When the family bought the house next door, they decided to build a new house and pool in its place. However, they ran into a problem. They had to move or tear down the old house. Some people wouldn't think twice about tearing down an old place, but the Hertz-Fong family wanted to see if someone could reuse it.

But finding someone who wanted to reuse the house proved to be very difficult. They tried to sell it on the Internet, but nobody wanted it. They tried to give it to a charity, but nobody would take it.

The family decided not to give up. Instead of tearing the old house down and throwing it into a landfill, they carefully took it apart. The reusable materials were pulled off and set aside, much of them suitable for reuse. For example, the doors and windows were sold to builders in Mexico. Once the old home had been completely cleared away, the family built their new house and pool.

Many architects are making an effort to reuse building materials in new buildings.

The Hertz-Fong family built their home out of both reused and recycled materials. If you look carefully at the concrete next to their sidewalk, you will see colored chips in it. The same chips appear in the tiles of their office bathroom. These chips are actually recycled items such as computer parts, buttons, old records, bits of plastic, and more. They have been mixed into a lightweight concrete material.

This material looks a lot like regular concrete, but it contains over 40% recycled material. Besides the areas already mentioned, the home also has countertops, bathtubs, showers, and patio floors made from the concrete material. Part of the pool is made from it, and so is the family's kitchen table.

The family also has a rooftop deck made from a special material. This material looks like wood, but it is actually a blend of natural and man-made products. To make it,

The family's rooftop deck is made of a material that blends plastic with recycled wood.

recycled wood and plastic are mixed together, with the plastic acting as a natural water **repellent**. The deck will last a long time, and it does not require chemicals to protect it from the weather.

As you can see, the Hertz-Fong house is special. The family has reduced its **consumption** of energy and water, as well as its use of chemicals for cleaning. They have also reused many types of materials, such as wood, dirt, and light fixtures, to construct a new home. And the family has built their kitchen, dining table, bathrooms, decks, and other items out of recycled materials.

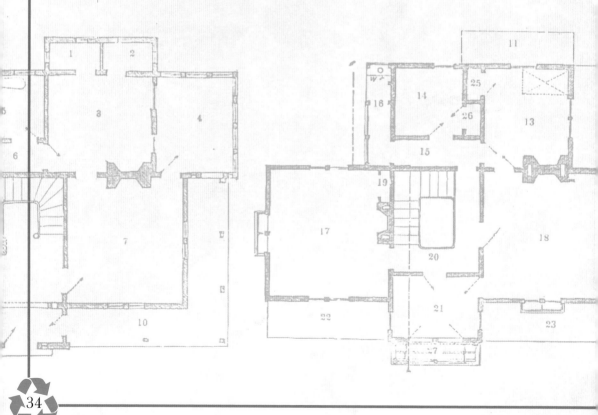

Ways You Can Reduce, Reuse, and Recycle

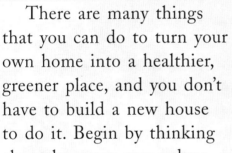

There are many things that you can do to turn your own home into a healthier, greener place, and you don't have to build a new house to do it. Begin by thinking about how you can reduce, reuse, and recycle.

Using less energy is a good place to start. Try letting in enough sunlight during the day so you don't need to use lights. Turn off lights when you leave a room, and never keep the television or computer on when they are not in use.

Besides reducing energy use, you can also reduce water consumption. The average U.S. family uses about 350 gallons of water a day—about the same amount of water that it would take to fill six or seven bathtubs. There should be plenty of ways for almost any family to **conserve** water.

Taking shorter showers is an easy place to start. If your shower sprays out four gallons a minute, staying in for ten minutes uses 40 gallons of water. Just think—you are pouring enough water to fill 76 two-liter bottles over your head during that 10-minute shower! Try cutting your shower time in half. You can also save water by turning off the faucet while brushing your teeth.

Playing with the garden hose on a hot summer day can be fun, but it can be a serious waste of water.

Reusing or recycling items around your house is another good way to make your household greener. For example, wash out an empty glass jar and use it for a pencil holder. When you outgrow clothes, donate them to a used clothing store. While you are at it, browse for some "new" clothes for yourself at the store. When you buy something really new, such as a pair of shoes, try to find a good use for the box. If you receive a package in the mail, save the packing for when you need to send something to someone else.

Ways to Reduce, Reuse, and Recycle

Reduce	Reuse	Recycle
Take shorter showers.	clothes	glass jars
Turn off lights, computers, and televisions when not in use.	goods (buy things like sports equipment, blankets, and book bags from thrift store)	newspapers, magazines, envelopes, cardboard
Shut off the water while brushing teeth.	packing material	plastic bottles
	school supplies	aluminum cans, aluminum foil
	glass jars, boxes	

Reusing school supplies is another great way to help Earth stay greener. Most students have some empty pages in their notebooks at the end of a school year. Instead of throwing your unused notebooks out, keep them for next year. Also, keep your folders, binders, pens, rulers, and other supplies in good shape so they can be reused. Getting the most use out of your supplies saves time, money, and energy—and it reduces waste.

Just like the Hertz-Fong family, you can reduce, reuse, and recycle to make your home a healthier and happier place. When you do, you make Earth healthier and happier, too.

Warm, bright, and Earth-friendly, the Hertz-Fong home can give us plenty of ideas for ways to build in the future.

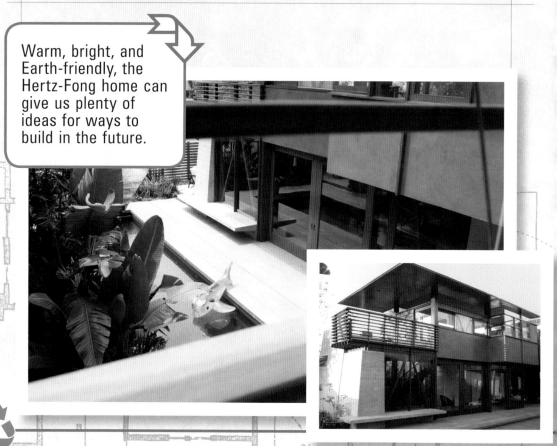

Glossary

atmosphere air that surrounds the earth

circulate flow around

conserve save

consumption use

convert change

funnel redirect

insulation material used to hold heat, electricity, or sound

ionizer device that uses electrical current to kill bacteria

landfill site where garbage is buried

microorganisms tiny living creatures that can sometimes
 be harmful

nonrenewable resources resources that cannot be replaced

ozone generator device that kills microorganisms by
 changing oxygen into ozone

photovoltaic changes light to electricity

radiant transferred through the air

repellent keeps something away

solar heat heat created by collecting energy from the sun

toxic poisonous

volatile organic compounds (VOCs) chemicals that give
 off fumes easily and have a sharp smell

Index